Nemidoonam
Nasim Rebecca Asl

VERVE
POETRY PRESS
BIRMINGHAM

PUBLISHED BY VERVE POETRY PRESS
https://vervepoetrypress.com
mail@vervepoetrypress.com

FIRST PUBLISHED FEB 2023

Printed and bound in the UK
by Imprint Digital, Exeter

ISBN: 978-1-913917-31-9

CONTENTS

Notes & Acknowledgements

Nemidoonam

For my mam, Hilary, and my
family - both blood
and found.

Zaban

My father's language is a house
I cannot enter. My teeth are strangers
to my tongue. It does not sit
or curl or roll as it should.
I cannot enter my dandaans. khareji
haunts my shadow. zaban-é pedar-é man
curls and rolls like birdsong I cannot mimic.
All my homes fall from my lips,
haunt my sayeh. I don't know
my father's language. nemidoonam
I say to aunts, cousins, uncles. I mime
all my khanehs. Falling from my lips,
motehasefam. I'm sorry. Forgive me,
nemidoonam. I mime to amoos, amays,
cousins with clenched dasts.
My family sips chai on scarlet carpets
they wove without me. motehasefam.
I'm sorry. Forgive me. baba, your language
is a home. My zaban can't shape its key.

Nemidoonam

I am alone in the living room when the phone rings.
I trudge across a Persian carpet to answer.
Pistachio flowers swallow my toes. I've been practicing
all week for this; greeting myself in the bathroom mirror,
looking for the stranger within my skin. I pick up the phone.
My ear is swallowed by a torrent of Farsi: *salaam. salaam amay.*

                                  salaam azizam.
             chetoree?
                         kheili khoob merci.
             khoobee? I try

The melon stand misses you, I think she says.
It doesn't taste the same when you're not here.
A continent away I can smell the anar on her breath.
She must be telling me about taking my cousins
to the park last night, how they threw the toop
between them as they went.

                      toop I say
                            toop, balé she replies

The plastic feels heavy against my head. I try not
to hear the voice that tells me she deserves more
than this neem-rooni. She watches me
from the wall and says   *baba? baba koo?*

                                 baba nist

I pretend to consider her reply, before I tell her:

nemidoonam. nemidoonam.

Okay she says. *Okay*

khodahafez I offer

dooset daram

she tells me. I say sorry to the dial tone. I know
she will try again later. Tonight, I will practice
my greetings again and one day, I think,
they'll stick.

Den-dwelling cubs

Before sunset my brother and I foraged for tools.
On tiptoes he gathered supplies like bundles of wood: toys,
lamps, pillows all spilling from the shoots of his arms.
I struck gold in the warm hollow of the airing cupboard
and brought him our mother's favourite cotton sheet.
Our hands worked quickly to reassemble his bedroom,
rebuilding our cavern under his desk. Silence nestled
between us. Cushions strewn like leaves in a forest
were our thrones. The smell of Persil dripped like rain
over our grass-stained knees. We drowned out the thunder
of our father with the crinklerustle of cheese and onion crisps.
Roosted under a canopy of fairylights, warmed by the glow
of Nintendo DS, I read books to him in whispers. We curled together
in sleep, our arms small enough to hold each other's dreams.

Exfoliation

The razor dances on my skin cross up scratch   missed a spot, back; one
leg stares, soft young clean. Goodbye dark hairs that dare to tumble from
Asian limbs

      [I was 11 when I stole my father's razor for the first time.

              (blue bic kiss on virgin skin

                try and fit in)].

Plastic beads storm the beach my body makes when it hits the water
press gently on my side hug my hips like an annoying child. Hello beauty
goodbye dead skin. Little corps   of me shake cry flake, spin spin sink
          into waves.

What had they seen, these microscopic mes? I hope they got to know the
world and not just the blade that severed them   from   the   loving   arms
of my calf. What had they seen? I remember reading   once   that it takes
the human body seven years to renew every single cell, which means that
one day   this body will not be the body branded by bruises

          (I can't bring myself to remember)

I won't count the rosary with my scars. I won't be in a body that once   loved
him and approximately 1,471   days from now he will be a stranger in more
than just a name. My limbs won't miss   missing him but that doesn't
explain the hurt I feel when blood balloons   at the razor's touch   soreness
that says a heart has   missing   parts. I look at my hands eventually
these hands will not be the hands that held my mother. These fingers will
not have stroked my dying grandma's hair. I don't want to wake up one day
and not see their shadows on my skin. Can I stop an exodus? I know there
are thoughts that go deep   into the body and weep, seep
      into sinew twine into the marrow of bones

        [they say trauma's inherited in DNA]

can't be shorn away but still I don't recognise memories of all the different incarnations of myself. In the quiet moments of the dark I scrape peel pull pluck away layers of all the girls I know I've been. Some cells thrive in me that I think are poisoned but I'd rather blame my shell than my soul and all the while

                                        my old skin
                        still
                                spirals

                        down
                the
        sink

Across from me, my mam

Laughter at the smell of joojeh kabob, spices
she now calls familiar, home in this strange city.
Her hand wraps around the wine stem

like my infant fingers once held hers.
We toast the mezze's arrival and she tells me, again,
of how she found my name: for nine days she pecked

at Persian books, bland sandwiches, slops of soup
splashing on hospital trays. She salted foreign sounds
over the incubator, her Mackem tongue stumbling

with each new letter and her newborn baby's brittle breaths.
Machinery hummed, her mint gown danced, when, finally,
she whispered her chosen name over my sleeping head.

Now, a breadstick dipped in Shiraz, she tells me
why I suit the syllables: *You are a breath
of fresh air. My summer breeze.* Now, still silent

I smile back. Sip. Don't ask if she regrets her choice.
All the storms that have seeped from me
have been mopped from our Persian carpets by her hand.

I have been a hormonal hurricane, a lost tsunami
racing, raging, door to door. I birthed tornados that ripped
through the fragile quiet of her home. Now, three decades later,

fissures are gathering in the porcelain of her face.
She wears it well, this evidence of her ageing. With each
new season she kneels by the bath, bows her head

over acrylic and stains herself with henna. Coaxes life
back into her hair. Last week I texted her a photo of the first
silver strand I plucked from mine. I don't have any dye

but she told me not to worry. Now, in this restaurant
the shadows of my empty arms stretch across the table
as she offers me her last kabob.

The meaning of my name

Nasim: Here we have the winds of summer lassoed into letters. You will arrive unannounced to bloom carnations on a stranger's dusty cheeks and allow the pink of their blood to dance. A welcome addition to the driest of days. A relief for parents used to a firstborn's sirocco and hurricane gale. You are temporal. Altruistic. Zephyr. Comfort bringer. You are a wordeater (just like your mam), a force of nature, a racoon-eyed windflower of a girl. You were serenaded by aeolian machines for the first nine nameless days of your life. Tubes billowed breath into your miniature lungs. It may take a while for the gust to carry you to yourself. For you to learn to breathe alone. Despair not - you are imbued with meaning.

For more famous Nasims please see: Pedrad, where comedy cancels the immigrant experience; Prince, where violence is performative; or Shah, a shadow who goes by the more pronounceable Naz.

we are nine and playing princesses

arms spiralling like sycamore seeds
we careen from one end of the big yard to the next.
grey pleats fan from our empty hips like ballgowns.

scalloped socks slide down our tiny ankles.
the plaits trailing behind our pigtailed heads are budding wings.
if we lay down in our shadows we'd be dwarfed.

you decree so we spin and spin and spin and spin until
grass is sky and clouds are daisies. we tumble,
flushed, limbs skidding on tarmac, knees grazed, breathless.

on bruised elbows i cross my legs to look at you.
when the war cry breaks out our classmates scatter like dandelion seeds.
i make a wish, then we're up and running from the yard

across the field, down the hill away, away from the power
of the boys nipping at our small heels. i am faster than you,
a berry-brown waif already used to fleeing the rumbling of a man.

your fingers stretch for mine. i pull you behind me.
ignore my bursting heart, the mess of moths rising
in the dust of my stomach i can't catch my breath

but as i turn to your buttercup hair my chin is glowing -
you are the most beautiful thing my short life has seen.
i don't know what this means. i release your milk-bottle fingers,

let a boy with hair as gold as yours snatch you instead.
i'm glad that he's not old or bold enough to pucker up.
your lips stay apple-red.

after school, i open my snow white diary
write *i'm scared i might love girls*, re-read my unjoined letters,
bury them in felt tip, slam shut the book, and feed it

to the monsters under my bed

Baba and the rhubarbstalk

I am five again. Curls plaited. Berry brown,
watching from the kitchen window as storm clouds
shroud the garden. Our rhubarb patch grows wild
in the northwest corner. It is my baba's pride and joy,
sown from seeds gifted by my mam.
Cumulonimbus conspire then strike – a flash
of hot-white lightning bolts through the plant.
My father bursts from the inside of a smoking stem,
eyes wild like the first man Mashya. He kneels.
Grasps half-torn leaves, cradles fragments
of cultivated homeland in his palms. He whimpers.

Then the whole plant shifts - stems groan, shoot skyward,
child-sized, car-sized, house-sized, taller, taller.
Taller. Baba stands before a beanstalk straight to the heavens.
The rhubarb ploughs past the moonstation, the starstation, past
the sunstation, on and on until the firmament fissures.
A figure appears.   I squint.
Mamanbozorg sits at the top of the stalks. She waves
a tiny hand at me. My father glances back, then up
towards his loss. He starts to climb, clambers leaf to leaf,
sweat pouring from his sunburnt skin.

With each new hand and foothold a piece of himself
plummets back to earth – I watch, helpless,
as my siblings tumble past. My mam floats down
to catch them. Streams of factory jobs drop
from his arms. Hardhats. Hi vis. Steel-capped shoes that fall in a flurry.
The BMW he always dreamed of is shaken from his hair.
A terraced house in South Shields, a dingy London flat.
John Denver and Googoosh cassettes. My poor dead uncle.
Lost false teeth. Sixty birthdays. His sisters left in Tehran,
all their tumours, years spent in uniform on the ocean,
the cypress tree from his childhood home, all drip
from his pockets. Memories flood the garden.
They lap against the patio, rising up our walls.
Still, baba   climbs
                climbs
        climbs
He reaches for his mother. She catches him
as the sky closes behind them.
My window shatters. Palms bleeding
I stagger among the debris of his life.
At my feet the rhubarb shrinks back into a bulb.
I look up at the fleeing clouds
then back down towards my loss.

Before the crossing

I have doused myself in salt and planted chrysalises of the ocean
into my cracked palms. Seaweed sewn into the crooks of my arms
tickles my elbows. Rain beams in my direction. One by one the pellets

hammer the swaddling tarp. *Let me in* they shout and don't take no
for an answer. Drizzle drips on my sleeping bag like starlight.
An orange jacket winces under my head. My fingers explore the cave

of canvas lent to me by a ghost. Left hand thumbs the firmament, traces
faded letters; right thumb strokes the streaks of ash I've shed
each morning. Two centimetres from my face the cedars are screaming.

Their emerald shrouds the stars. Ebony eyes squint through the darkness.
Half-shadowed squatting boys murmur psalms over a gas stove
the size of a sandal. Behind them huddles the final bag of basmati.

This last night I dream of my mother in a kitchen 4,064km away, plucking
feathers from a flotilla of carcasses, checking the news for me each day.

#DatingWhileBrown

Tinder message received July 2018:

> *sells himself to ethnically ambiguous girl*
> 'I once ate bombay mix at a Nisa's'

a strange man typed / then sent / alarm emojis ring in my head / it's 1:04pm / maybe he has ghazā on the brain, racked his mind to try and find the ingredients / of my DNA / I blink / blink / blink / the scorpion wrapped around my heart stings my left cheshm / tail thrashing against my skull in rage / breathe in out / beh / khārej / I unleash my hands / let my fingers paint pixel symphonies / to explain away my brown / dō bloodlines wrap around the caduceus of my body / these veins are not mârha at war / I am Simurgh / copper feathers streaming from my scalp / I want to tell him he has picked the wrong region / that my people are herby / I stew / we stew / they stew / pots of sabzee / I taste my heritage with an English tongue / I try to tell him I have not visited a Nisa since I ran out of mixer / at a mehmooni in an old friend's flat / I bought some Walker's Sensations / along with the own-brand lemonade / I definitely paid in pounds / they don't accept the rials that I don't know how to count / I want to tell him I hung the flag of Iran above my hi-fi when I was twelve / beside my *Mizz Magazine* Nick Jonas shrine / that esfand burned in my yellow bedroom / smoke curling into waves / I want to tell him that John Denver blasted from my speakers / the vibrations shaking the green white red / sabz sefeed ghermez / I want to tell him this album is my baba's favourite / that in our house my mam's Geordie dastam make the best chayee / I type:

> there is nothing ambiguous / about my dual existence /
> delete the message / then remove him from my zendegi /

Bia, Zayanderud, bia

Bia breath-bringer. Life-giver. Plant-creator.
Bia soil-quenching Zayanderud. Bia.
Can you hear us begging for you,
on our knees in your parched grave?
Our hopes have keeled
with our grandfathers' boats.
Wooden corpses rotting
in the sun. Our children pluck
fishbones like lice
from your cracked clay.
The cragged planks of their bodies
are spelks in our hearts. Eyes too dry for tears,
did you spy them pocketing sundrenched
darics and ancient, moonwept rials when
our backs were turned? All those wishes
running dry. Bia Zayanderud, bia.
Can you feel our legs thumping
on your chest, our farmer army crying
for your return? For you to feed.
To heal. To clean. We will take up
arms to free you from the officed men
who've claimed you for themselves,

they who've robbed our arid land
the turquoise jewel of you. Break
through the dams that prison you, rust the
pipes that cage you now below our feet.
Trapped in the dark, we alone still
hear you weep. Bia, Zayanderud, bia.
Do you listen to our whispered secrets
or taste the sweat we bead for you
like tasbih, when we settle for the night in your
empty bed? Can you sense the way
we rise like herons, our
restlessness at dawn?

Can you hear our pulses beat
with our marching sandals? Can you feel it
when the uniformed unleash their daily
torrent; are you stained too when
their bullets drench us red?

Can you smell the iron pang
of the blood we leak back
into your belly? Can
you taste this – the
hopelessness
of prayer
?

As we depart my fatherland

the unveiling begins. A tidal wave of hands cascades through the cabin,
stretching to the ceiling. Manicured fingers held to foreheads,
just like dua. Just like farewell. Scarves slip from scalps.

Row after row of ebony crops, acorn-brown plaits,
anar-red bobs, chemical-straight peroxide,
henna, all bloom at the ping of the seatbelt sign.

I release my curls from their shroud. They flow
to my shoulders and frizz with delight. I unleash
my clavicle, let it drink conditioned air that tickles

just like a lover's lips. Like this. Unafraid now, I greet
myself. Stroke again this evidence of my skeleton,
this fragile bone that bridges my body's east and west.

Far below us, a woman dreams of hairstyles no stranger
will see. She looks to the sky, mistakes our plane for satellite
or star. A vapour trail of guilt follows me home.

A resurrection in north-west Iran

Mamanbozorg splits threads in the Caspian sun. We hear again
her rusted tongue speak, weave, paint carpets Persian. Here again,

the lambs she lambed raise their heads at the sound of her song.
Her roosari dances. She calls to a God who answers, and cheers again:

Golgaz. Sweet flowers shed thorns and burst through dry soil to
carpet her feet. Sunlight holds her. She won't disappear again.

Under a pall of flour, she kneads. Births noon and cherry wine.
Saffron, rose and thyme crescendo in her mouth. She feels again,

moves to the city where her children grew with the mountains.
Dusk breaks. She toddles the ninis to the park. Happy tears again.

She crosses the world and wonders if it's faith keeping the plane
adrift. A runway of stars leads her to us. The skies clear again.

Baba gets a chance to say goodbye but won't. Not again. She makes
space for me beside her and says "Nasim, bia inja" - Come here, again.

A kaleidoscope oscillates in Aberdeen, 2019

On this island, where only creatures blessed with wings
can migrate, I once was caught in a tornado of
Painted Ladies. Mid-run, round the back of
Kittybrewster Pure Gym, the kaleidoscope
descended, dripping through June like
marmalade. Tigers clustered in
honeyed air. Tangerines.
Bronze battalions.
Insects claiming
a patch of grass
they must
have thought
a mirage or heaven.
One drank from my sweatdrowned
skin. Tapped a rhythm so quick I couldn't
translate, its hindlegs clinging to the stubble of
my arms, all my outer margins. It ignored my heaving
diaphragm, the grin leaking from my cheeks into
afternoon, how my fingers fluttered as I went to
touch its thorax. Brown and soft and fragile
as my throat. I waited on the roadside,
held my arm high and still and solid,
like a branch, a regret, a promise,
until the passing congregation
beat again their fiery halves.
Some rumpled, missing

legs, all drunk on
knapweed,
ragwort
I'd never
noticed, thistles
planted by the council.
They clouded their sky anew.
Swirled away. I ran again eventually,
the monochrome city greyer now than
it had ever been before. Sunblushed, eyelids
lusty red with light, I let Siri lead me back to the
flat I stayed in, mountainless roseless Rosemount
Street where my books lay like pupa on the floor.
I charged uphill, as though I too was flying towards the pull
in my gut, crossing seas, hills, deserts, valleys, gullies, lakes,
rivers, puddles, streams, cities, towns, pebbles, motorways, forests,
garden centres, sandgrains, roads, seaglass, driftwood, waypaths,
borders, housing estates, power plants, pylons, fields, ruins,
and streets and streets and streets, as though I too could
just fly back to my beginnings, halfway around the world.

I teach table manners to hedgehogs

I'm having tea with hedgehogs
in my mam's garden. Little claws
tap tap tapping against chai glasses
each time they take a sip.
Around my favourite sofreh, a web-white island
in too-long grass, we are cross-legged,
drowsy with nabot, our lips and snouts
dewy with honey, saffron and sugar.
When I pour the teapot tadpoles gush
from the spout. Grunts echo around me.
When I serve snails on slimy side plates,
I tell the hedgehogs off for chattering too loud.
I know it is their instinct to celebrate their riches
but I'm afraid of what the neighbours will think
of their ululations. We already smell
too strange for this street - sickly rose,
tangy like turmeric, heady with cardamom.
Cinnamon is not desirable all year round.
I explain this to my hedgehogs as they silently
clamp sugar cubes between their teeth.
I count their spines with teaspoons,
tell them back their names – hedgehog,
joojeh teeghee. That translates as blade-birds,
but they shrug when I ask how they lost their wings.
They ripple like a field of wheat
as I stroke them, marvelling at how
they wear their armour so boldly,
these glorious spiky mice, when my own back
is bare flesh ridged with longing.

I don't tell my hedgehogs that beyond
these fences their species is on the decline,
that when I return home and drive again
through memory, their corpses litter the roads.
I avert my gaze from the bloodied beaks
of seagulls who have swarmed inland
to slurp the innards of my friends.

Here, around our oldest sofreh,
my hedgehogs only murmur now
when I offer them some slugs.
Here, among our daisies and hyacinths,
in my mam's garden, my hedgehogs
are quiet, living.

Translating بابا

As noun: Male caregiver, parent, progenitor. Dad. Daddy. Pops. Papa. Pa. Dada. Old man. Father, though not a substitute for God.

As beginning: Babies say بابا in their first canonical stages of babble. When babies build towers with tongues, shape bricks with lips and burst air through throats to communicate, trying to bind breath with meaning, بابا is one of the first accidental sounds they birth. Second often – though not always – to mam.

As assimilation: بابا on the Tehran metro. بابا in bazaar بابا at Imam Khomeini International Airport. بابا on arrival, at departure, collecting baggage, to deny the burgundy of your passport, to earn your crowning veil, to become no one in the humid streets, to be unremarkable to the watermelon sellers and cobblers.

As sound: Pay attention to the plosive. Buh buh. Buh buh buh buh. Buh. In this alliterative barrage you will find your father. Multiple bs are used to emphasise harshness, sow discord, bamboozle, unsettle. In بابا the bs are split by arhs that try to soften the blow. It doesn't always work.

As inheritance: I have my بابا's russet eyes. Honey in the Caspian sun. Onyx on our thunder days. The shape of my skull mirrors his own. My sister writes with his hand: my mam's failing eyes can no longer tell their script apart. My brother stole his posture, his kidney stones, the scratch of his beard. Both their jaws wired shut in blaring silence. What do we take from our باباs? Do we always need more than they can give?

As learning: As in بابا آب داد. The first sentence small hands learn to write
                                                                      left to Right
Dad gave water. Where داد almost sounds like dad, almost
like father, almost like بابا. Some بابا s are بابا at home, in
childhood, but dad outside. In بابا آب داد fathers are split
across their own offering, the water, this balance.

As affection: بابا is not used only for بابا s. As a term of endearment, it's
not uncommon to hear friends call each other بابا or for
parents to بابا their own children. We're all fathering each
other. بابا here is a less scary word for love. In Iran, my بابا
بابا s without abandon, baptises a battalion of بابا s,
summoning his image in everyone he meets.

As respect: بابا for the man cooking corn on Valiasr Avenue. بابا for the
taxi driver. بابا for the kebab maker in the café beside the
house. بابا can also be used for strangers, though آقا
is preferred.

As interjection:: Ay بابا. As in: oh man, oh boy, oh jeez. For when you miss
a turn, drop a glass, believe a bombshell, forget a word you
know in another language. Berate yourself. Blame your
father. Ayبابا. A reminder of all the mistakes we know we
shouldn't make.

One Wednesday in our first November

I fill your room with candles, surprise electronic bulbs
planted onto polyester. The hyponychium of my right thumb
hums. I flicked them all by hand. Twilight rustles your blinds
as I wait like Sita, nestled in a runway of jewels, a firefly
fluttering with the stars. We sit among the diyas
and compare our cognates:

chai, paneer, naan,
safed, narenji, rang,

(we decide darling sounds the same)

dō, hamesha, andar,
dur, shayad, khali

When we exhaust our zaban you retreat. One by one
I extinguish our artificial suns. You ebb back to night;
I watch you disappear through the window. Refound moonlight
strokes my cheek. I gown myself in ruby sheets that smell like you,
awake until dawn, wondering how jaan and joon can sound so similar
when we have such different words for love.

Say begu

After Ocean Vuong

Say bia, sit doon, besheen, hoy ya jacket
on the bannister. Say salaam, bienvenue,
I'm welcome here, or khoshbakhtam. Say I dream
in a kaleidoscope of language.
Say aye, aray, bale, na, och ne way, ne chance,
ne bosh, nemidoonam. Say baba believes in aliens.
Say mam believes in angels. Say ah believe in nowt.
Say my orstokhan are knackered. Say slower please,
lotfan, s'il vous plait moins vite. Say yes.
Say motehasefam or bebakshid. Say boro, after you, allons-y, yallah.
Say all your brother's words. Say ya forgive ya sister.
Say you forgive yasel. Say you believe is.
Say FTM. Say I'll gan wherever you are.
Say dooset daram. Say je t'aime, te amo,
wo ai ni, say my eyes are galaxies, khoshgel.
Say I love you in as many zaban as you can muster
& when you run out say it in your own. Say sorry.
Say ---- is gone now. Say they didnae mean it. Say yal be areet.
Say ta, cheers, merci, mamnoon. Say thank you to ya mam.
Say ---- is an alcoholic. Say you propa miss them.
Say you miss me. Say all owa lies have led us here.
Say I didnae mean to be so radge. Say khoobam.
Mean it anarl. Say Allah, mon dieu, khodahafez, say God.
Say all me bairns are make-believe. Say my wishes are parvaneh.
Say you think about is often. Say you'll be okay.
Say befarmid. Say ya feel the same.
Say the truths I tell mesel are rivers.
Say hava do nafaras. Say your place is empty.
Say gan hyem. Say wor ---- is waiting.

Say al be khaneh before ya ken.
Say I'll meet me there.

An overdue apology for

jamming my little brother's finger
in the patio door of my grandparents' bungalow -
it must have been '98 or '99 (they were both alive).
I'm sorry for how loud he yowled,
how his hamstercheeks wobbled and contorted
his ink-bowled head as he cradled his hand
like a broken spider. His cry was purple.
He bawled like the moon. I'm sorry
it took a week for his mottled thumb
to ripen to perennial wallflower, to plum,
a bunch of Vitoria grapes, then sludge.

I'm sorry it took so long for nail
to peel away from digit, that it revealed
new flesh, pink, puckered, raw, never meant to be seen.
If he could have spoken
he'd have only said
how much he hurt.

Vignettes of acceptance

i

Night skies were once lit only by the moon's perfect grace and the flickering histories of constellations. Light from the past scattering in the atmosphere. Once we all had starglow skin. These are tales mothers whisper now to children who doze in beds built by a stranger's bloodied back. These are tales I will whisper to my unborn children as the yellow glare of lampposts leads us all to dreams. Tonight there is no howling moon. Above our bowed heads greed chokes the stars.

ii

Ribs protect the inner organs, the secret workings of the heart, the ferocious beat of the body. Mine have, at times, tried to burst through my flesh. Starvation once lured my skeleton to the surface. Shaking fingers traced those me-made mountains, tarnished crown to hungry hollow. All my jagged peaks. Passing pilgrims left meagre offerings - fruit, lips, fury - at the altar of my body. My bones have since retreated. I am soft now when I touch my chest. Sometimes I miss myself.

iii

Rootless hundreds have exploded into thousands, millions. Nomad. Wayfarer. Vagrant. Endless waves of ungrounded people weave through the news on their way to hostile worlds. I don't know how they find the hope to build shelter where once there was none. Blossoming tongues study the word for home in a foreign house. The somewhere their spirits long for is forever lost. It matters not that they bury their dead in soil they do not know the truth of; they know better than most that we are all equal in the gaping maw of the earth.

iiii

Otters sleep clasping paws so they can defy the tides and stay together.

I've made peace with the lull and pull of my body, the currents of doubt that flood my veins and curl the ends of my hair. Let me return to the river - to the pikes' sharp teeth, the high backs of roaches. I want to count the patchy scales of the carp. I am no longer scared of drifting away; when I sleep, my hands no longer feel empty without someone else to hold.

Fill in the (____)

After Regi Claire

You were _____ (15, 22, 31) and it was _____ (summer, February, yesterday). The _____ (sun, moon, stars) had risen. All was well. The sky was _____ (cold, dancing, blazing) and you were _____ (with friends, alone, waiting) in _____ (a club, public, the street), your _____ (trackies, dress, jeans) wearing you like a second skin. You were glowing in the light of _____ (mobiles, lampposts, strobes), you in all your _____ (olive, ivory, flushed) glory. I see you still, beautiful, bold, _____ (rainburnt, sweatdewed, starsprayed). The _____ (world, night, future) was yours if you dared to seize it.

He was _____ (your friend, your friend's friend, a stranger) when he saw you in _____ (a club, public, the street). You thought he was _____ (beautiful, kind, a creep), and told him so. You were _____ (tipsy, sober, drunk) and told him _____ (so, go, no). He was wearing _____ (trackies, jeans, a suit) and said you were _____ (beautiful, kind, a treat). He asked for _____ (your name, a dance, your number) then circled you like a _____ (shark, planet, final answer). You pretended he was invisible. In _____ (a club, public, the street, a room, the house, a bed) _____ (music, silence, time) was too loud. It beat with your heart.

You _____ (yelled, cried, can't remember). You _____ (froze, fought, kicked, panicked) as all your organs turned to stone. The sky was _____ (crying, yelling, jeering) at the two of you under its gaze. The world began again that _____ (autumn, April, night). That _____ (autumn, April, night) your feet learned how quickly _____ (sand, safety, hope) shifts beneath the weight of things we _____ (quietly, boldly, cannot) name. His _____ (wrists, shoulder blades, forearms) were _____ (strong, barbed, rough) against the softness of your flesh. He smelled like _____ (rain, sweat, your favourite aftershave). Your body felt like _____ (pain, betrayal, another's). Your bruises were _____ (moss, teeth, grapes) speckled like nebulae across your _____ (thighs, neck, chest). His voice was _____ (muffled, laughing, urgent) when he told you to _____ (relax, relax, relax).

You last saw him _____ (then, Thursday, the next day) in _____ (a club, public, the street). The _____ (stars, sun, moon) already _____ (setting, melting, mourning). He _____ (waved, ignored you, liked your photo on Instagram). Your breath _____ (flickered faltered, caught) like a _____ (lighter, hummingbird, mouse).

You know you cannot _____ (forgive, forget, relax).

Nini Khomkhomu

a fable among the people of Urmia

When I lived, their hisses slithered behind me.
Torshideh. Jendeh. My pickled hips an empty
promise. Soured. I loved and loved,
bedded and bedded, peeled open
my heart, my legs, again, again

trying to find my way to that other promised world.
To you, sweet bache, koochaloo. I was born to be maman.
I died with empty arms, degh kard, withered breasts,
all my unbroken waters still churning at my wellspring.

I cling to mountains as my unborn babies
should have clung to me. Earth shakes
when I sob. In the valley where my barren body
rotted, families grow to fear me.

In death their whispers call me Nini Khomkhomu.
Nightjars call warnings from Judas trees
when I wake with dusk. They cry like cicadas,
watchful as serpents, their stony feathers glaring.

Branches drizzle me with petals – soorati for my dohktar –
and blanket my path. My bare brown feet bloody.
I croon lullabies to the moon. Tulips bow as I pass.
Starstorms crown me silver. I glow white and bright
like sorrow among the trees when I hear it:

mewing, wailing, screaming. Answering the summons,
I blaze back to life, arrive at the side of a cradle
staring at a miracle. Its sleeping parents cannot hear her;
my new daughter weeps only for me. In my arms she settles,
fat fists in my hair. I drop a tear on her forehead.

My nini, baba, peri will never grow old. She clasps
my hand as we roam every forest, her siblings,
all rescued, all taken, all cherished, flocking around us,
squabbling like pigeons, trilling with larks and nightingales,
babbling with possibility. We dust ourselves in sumac,
the sun turmeric on our skin, we count eagles, owls,
the heavy-set bustards roaming our uplands,
we chant ka ka ka with the cuckoos as month after month
we find crib after crib. We rescue the babies
no one else will care for and I carry them all
- their futures, their talents, their promise -
balanced like love, heavying my hips.

Ode to Sinners, 63 Newgate Street

Here's to staying out past 2am
for the first time in three years.

Here's to floors awash with booze,
beer, vodka, mixer, sticking to our shoes.

Here's to bass drumming in our ribs,
to guitarbeats, remixes so loud we are pressed

like shells to each other's ears to shout secrets
no one else can hear. All the club's a stage.

Here's to toilet paper trains trailing heels
down the bathroom's aisle. Here's to sisterhood

in the ladies', to rants about men, to extolling the virtues
of strangers you'll never see again. Here's to dancing.

To exorcising adulthood, to hands that linger,
to our favourite singers emerging from the speakers

like Mithras from rock, Aphrodite rising from the sea
sloshing around our feet. Here's to blisters.

Here's to being too old for going out out. To yawns
that simmer at the shores of our lips, to constellations of sweat

glimmering on our philtrums. Here's to the cage
at the edge of all things, to the bodies still

slim enough to squeeze through the bars,
to the bright budgies writhing and thriving

and smiling inside, a melody of off-key seagulls
while their pals record videos that'll disappear

with morning. Here's to not caring your mascara has smudged.
Here's to being the youngest we'll ever be.

Here's to not being IDed. Here's to £2.50 trebs,
to apple-sour shots, to fingers that find each other

in the dark, to the dregs, to moonlight
spying on us past the guards at the doors.

Here's to illicit plastic straws. Here's to paparazzi
strobes documenting our indiscretions.

Here's to beginnings, crowds thinning, reason dimming,
here's to bringing the moves. Here's to jackets

tied like ballgowns around our waists. Here's to him
for spinning you away from the leches. Here's to grinning

against stubbled cheeks, to tiptoes and aching Achilles,
to skin grazing, to winners, to grace, to the small back of midnight,

to coats exchanged to keep you warm, to stinging mouths,
to ears ringing for dawn, to the firefly glow of your last cigarette.

Here's to the drunken wings we grow. Here's to your feathers,
to how soft and light and tipsy their promise feels in my arms.

I should be stepping off a train at Central Station

Instead I sip chayee in my flat. My fingers hold
each other around the glass. A travel mug watches
from the kitchen counter, comforted by a blanket of dust.
Sundrops reach in and pat my thigh.

Clouds meander. I squint at the cumulus
and in their shapes I see the trowel I know
is cradled in my mother's hands, the silver tool
submerging and emerging in and from the earth.

Last summer, standing under a mackerel sky, we spotted
dolphins dancing along the North East coast.
I think of the thrill of finding them amongst the grey,
how quickly she snapped her binoculars to look.

Today she kneels in the grass. Her hands browned,
mud speckling her fingers, inspecting row upon row
of new beginnings – tomatoes, raspberries, mint.
Constellations of freckles blossom on her shoulders.

I ask the sky to give her shade and hope that,
150 miles south east, clouds will spread their wings
to shield her as she transplants her first spring shoots
from rusted pot to soil.

She makes a mental note to tell me, next time she calls, of this:
the new life born from her hands. I sense her success,
settle back into black cracked leather and drink the tea
she taught me to make the last time we spoke.

Backgammon by the Caspian Sea

Makeshift sofreh strewn between us, we unfold our board,
       plant walnut into beach. You divide the stones inherited
from our unmet bababozorg. I bear off my roosari,

hoist my manteau to my elbows, ignore your finger twitching
       at the sight of my wrist's bare flesh drinking dawn.
The next move is yours. A chadored blot on this shrinking shoreline,

face furrowed like sand, a smirk escapes you as dice explode
       from your shaking fist. You counterplay with tasbih, each orb
a drop of sun you roll between your fingers. The sky blushes orange.

A whispered breeze nibbles the clouds; on the slopes behind us
       oriental beech, juniper, and cypress trees all cheer. Our pieces
dance across the wood. We pretend not to see sanderlings

starving behind our shadows or eagle owls brooding
       in the boarded ruins of a bar. Egrets and coots
squawk and grunt like men in the bazaar.

Your fist clenches fabric that swirls heart-height.
       I comb the ghost-sand, find shell after shell after shell,
scavenged treasures I crush to my ears. Check. Swing.

Shake from them: azan, a last call to breakfast,
       memories of waves rolling at our feet. You press on,
pass me, cheeks flushed at the power you clutch in your hand.

Your russet eyes celebrate victory. I fold my chips back
       into the vanishing sea. Resign. Reveil. Rerobe. Reward you my roosari,
hold still and let you mould again the white cotton to my face.

Dearly beloved

When you are gathered here, one day, accept this codicil.
I hope by now my chattels will have been distributed – yes, I hear
my bangles singing on your wrist. I wish to split
my greatest gift: the miracle that is my body, my soulcage, me.
Will my executor please step forward? This skin
is my estate. I leave behind no bricks or mortar.
I just have this – the mountain ranges of my body.
Swan arms, legs of willow. Inherit me.

I'll let the court of protection take it from here, but know
my spirit will be sitting in a theatre seat as the troupe
of scrubs pluck organs like bulbs from my body.
I will cheer when the scalpel slices my skin
and the first kidney is squelched from within.
Know I'll throw roses at the sight of my secrets sitting
in a row of blue boxes. Distribute them in the night.
Leave my heart for last.
Alas, beloved – proof it exists! Now give it to a girl
bound by tubes to a hospital bed.
Silence the machines beeping her funeral march.
Give her my encore: I will beat in her chest.

Burn my residue. Leave me my eyes; they'll bubble,
break from my face when the fire takes hold.
I am afraid of the dark. Return half my bones
to my father's land so I can straddle the worlds
I couldn't bridge with my flesh. I want to be scattered
at the Caspian Sea, to see the sun crescent as I dissolve
into oblivion. I want to be snowsift in Tehran, to melt
into Damavand's twisting streams and nurse
the burning feet of babies swaddled in the shade.

I want my other half to rest: my knees, my chin, my thighs.
Bury what's left in the alcove where my grandparents lie.
I'll mix with their memories, ash and ash. Dust sharing space.
In pieces we will spend eternity counting stars above our heads
in the town that birthed us all.

Beloved,   please visit.
   Bring me marigolds
on my birthday.   Take time.
Blanket my plaque in petals.   Kneel.
          Bask in the last of my presence.
   Wipe the rust from my lettering. Tell me   about your day.
          I want to meet your children.
Then, beloved, I will happily
                                                  wane away.

Heirlooms

This body is an archive / birthmark above my right ear hidden by the chestnut vines of my hair / I will let you peel back this curtain / and kiss me / here / where my skull is softest / I don't know if this marks the spot where my other lovers used to kiss me / or if it reveals how I died / in my last life / there's no one left / to speak for the forest of my scalp / I have my mam's square chin / her love of words / I parrot my sister's giggle / the wringing of her hands / my grandma's front teeth could fit in my gums / in photos we wear the same awkward grace / bones too big for our bodies / broad / I held her ivory hand when she passed / her skin a butterfly's wing / translucent / I carry her wedding ring around my neck / and leave my left hand bare / all the women who birthed me could fit under the clavicle of the sky / my eyebrows / patience / yearning / meet in the middle of my face / my tastebuds have abandoned their tolerance for spice / my brain is a museum / where footage of breakups is played on an infinite loop to tired spectators / every single tumble / all my muddled words / nails strong for peeling pomegranates / splitting threads / when I am still / I feel ghost spiders / fingers / fangs / marching on my chest / my childhood imagination lurks between my toes / I am looking for what it means to belong / my great-grandmother's rapist / haunts our family tree / her copy of Little Women sits on my bookshelf / this body is a graveyard / I have shed hairs in more places than I'll ever know / spilled skincells like breadcrumbs across the earth / I've seen more of this planet than those who came before / my eyes belong to my ancestors / my face has all the features / of everyone they ever loved / I am a mashup of all their longing / their mistakes / fleshy hips tight with trauma / passed through the mother's water / the mother's water / the mother's water / all our puddles drink the moon / saline / bangles chime in my bones / willowed fingers made for weaving carpets / sew instead with pens / ink pools in my unbroken waters / my body does not yet know / what it will give to its daughter
/ I will never know / what her daughters / will take from us /

New roots

Love, I am planting new roots with you.
Our hands speckled with muddy constellations

as we sit cross-legged and dig.
Love, look at how our tendrils seek

new earth, twining together
in knots our gentle fingers

can't untangle alone. Love,
see how we're growing together.

We spend our weeks and months watching
the radicle anchoring. We smile with one mouth

as the first small shoots push through dark
to light. Love, we'll take turns

to feed and water & when our tree reaches the sky, stretches
for the stars, we will sit under boughs laden with blossom

& marvel at what we have created. This life.
Love, we know some storms are forecast,

that there'll be winds we cannot predict,
that rain will brew on our horizon -

but we will bandage each snapped branch,
will gather every fallen twig, mend and monitor any cracks.

Love, we know passing clouds can never topple us.
Love, we know how deep our tender roots have grown.

GLOSSARY

amay	Paternal aunt	*hamesha*	Always
amoo	Paternal uncle	*hava do nafaras*	Weather is meant for two
anar	Pomegranate		
andar	Inside	*jaan/joon*	Darling
aray	Yes	*jendeh*	Slut, whore
azan	Call to prayer	*joojeh kabob*	Chicken kebab
azizam	My darling	*joojeh teeghee*	Hedgehog
baba	Dad	*khali*	Empty
bababozorg	Grandfather	*khaneh*	Home/house
baché	Child	*kharej*	Out
balé	Yes	*khareji*	Foreigner
bebakshid	Excuse me	*kheili khoob*	Very good
befarmid	Go ahead	*khodahafez*	Goodbye
begu	Say	*khoobee*	How are you
beh	In	*khoshbakhtam*	Welcome
besheen	Sit down	*khoshgel*	Beautiful
bia inja	Come here	*koo*	Where
boro	Go	*koochaloo*	Little one
chai/chayee	Tea	*lotfan*	Please
cheshm	Eye	*mamanbozorg*	Grandmother
chetoree	How are you?	*mamnoon*	Thank you
dandaan	Teeth	*manteau*	Modest coat
dast	Hand	*mârha*	Snakes
degh kard	To die from heartbreak	*Mashya*	The first man in Persian mythology
dō	Two	*mehmooni*	Party
dokhtar	Daughter	*motehasefam*	I'm sorry
dooset daram	I love you	*nabot*	Crystallised sugar
dua	Prayer	*naan*	Bread
dur	Distant	*narenji*	Orange
esfand	Rue seeds, burnt to ward off evil eye	*neem-rooni*	Half-Iranian
		nemidoonam	I don't know
ghazā	Food	*nini*	A young child
ghermez	Red	*nist*	Not here

orstokhan	Bones
paneer	Cheese
parvaneh	Butterfly
peri	Fairy-like being
rang	Colour
roosari	Headscarf
sayeh	Shadow
sabz	Green
sabzee	Vegetables
safed/sefeed	White
shayad	Perhaps
Simurgh	Mythological bird
sofreh	Cloth used as table
soorati	Pink
tasbih	Prayer beads
torshideh	Unmarried woman
toop	Ball
zaban	Language/Tongue
zaban-e pedar-e man	My father's language
zendegi	Life
بابا	Baba, Dad
بابا آب داد	Dad gave water

ACKNOWLEDGEMENTS

Thanks to my mam, Hilary, for her love, support, and guidance in every aspect of my life. This collection is for her, and for my grandma, Edna. Thank you both for giving me your love of words.

All my love and gratitude to those who have sat through countless open mics to offer their friendship, especially Rachel Coburn, Adam Murdoch and Colin Abercrombie. Thanks too to the friends who have engaged and cheered from afar, especially Daniel Lawson, Abby Picken and Simon Lindsley. Thank you to Hazel Mirsepasi for finding the perfect pomegranates.

My biggest thanks must go to those who have curated the spaces in which most of these poems were birthed. Thank you to the Scottish BPOC Writers Network for their endless opportunities. Thanks to Alycia Pirmohamed for bringing me into the fold, and your advice and support ever since. Nadine Aisha Jassat – thank you for your mentorship and friendship and for opening this world back up to me when I thought I'd left it behind. Thank you Hannah Lavery, for your friendship, your laughs and for curating endless wonderful workshops. Thanks to Steve Dearden and the Writing Squad for their constant belief in me and for the opportunities they've given me to grow as a writer. Thanks to Kevin P. Gilday for your feedback, friendship and generosity, and for the Scribblers Union. Thank you to the Scottish Book Trust for your support and for pairing me with Cynthia Miller – thank you, Cynthia, for making me a better poet.

Thanks to those who have looked at iterations of this manuscript and the poems within and offered invaluable feedback – Juana Adcock and the Poetry Translation Centre, Ross McWhinnie, Leigh-Anne Brown, Kate Smith and Charlotte Johnson.

Many thanks too to the editors who gave many of these poems their first homes. 'Zaban' and 'Translating Baba' in *Poetry Wales*;

'Nemidoonam' in *Fringe of Colour Films*; Scottish BPOC Writers Network for including 'Den-dwelling cubs' and 'we are nine and playing princesses' in your Writers of Colour Audio Anthologies and for including 'Exfoliation' and 'A Resurrection in North West Iran' in the Tapsalteerie Press pamphlet *Ceremony*; 'Vignettes of Acceptance' in *The Dark Horse Magazine*; 'Before the Crossing' in *Gutter Magazine*; '#DatingWhileBrown' in *Middleground Magazine*; 'As we depart my fatherland' as part of Ripples of Hope Festival 2021, with thanks to The Writing Squad; 'Dearly Beloved' and 'I should be stepping off a train at Central Station' were both in *Not About Now, a Writing Squad Anthology 2021* and were written alongside Lydia Allison; 'The meaning of my name' and 'Heirlooms' in the *Glasgow Women Library's Responders of Colour Annual 2022*.

ABOUT VERVE POETRY PRESS

Verve Poetry Press is a quite new and already award-winning press that focussed initially on meeting a local need in Birmingham - a need for the vibrant poetry scene here in Brum to find a way to present itself to the poetry world via publication. Co-founded by Stuart Bartholomew and Amerah Saleh, it now publishes poets from all corners of the UK and beyond - poets that speak to the city's varied and energetic qualities and will contribute to its many poetic stories.

Added to this is a colourful pamphlet series, many featuring poets who have performed at our sister festival - and a poetry show series which captures the magic of longer poetry performance pieces by festival alumni such as Polarbear, Matt Abbott and Genevieve Carver.

The press has been voted Most Innovative Publisher at the Saboteur Awards, and has won the Publisher's Award for Poetry Pamphlets at the Michael Marks Awards.

Like the festival, we strive to think about poetry in inclusive ways and embrace the multiplicity of approaches towards this glorious art.

https://vervepoetrypress.com
@VervePoetryPres
mail@vervepoetrypress.com